TWELVE SCENIC WALKS

around the

YORKSHIRE DALES

by

J.Brian Beadle

GW00707762

Number two in the
Trailblazer 'Scenic Walks' series

1

First published in Great Britain in 2000 by Trailblazer Publishing (Scarborough)

ISBN 1 899004 33 5

Trailblazer Publishing (Scarborough)
Stoneways
South End
Burniston
Scarborough. YO13 0HP

MAPS
The maps in this book are not to scale and are for guidance only. They do not accurately portray the right of way. It is the readers responsibility not to stray from the right of way and it is strongly advised that you take the relevant Ordnance Survey map with you on the walk.

WARNING
Whilst every effort has been made for accuracy neither the publisher nor the author bear responsibility for the alteration, closure or portrayal of rights of way in this book. It is the readers responsibility not to invade private land or stray from the public right of way for walkers. All routes in the book should be treated with respect and all precautions taken before setting out. Any person using information in this book does so at their own risk.

Cover Picture: Tree growing through limestone pavement near Grassington photographed by the author

2

CONTENTS

DEATH AT THE STRID!

A 'strid' is a section of fast flowing water where the river is forced into a narrow channel usually through rocks. When the river is in flood the thunderous torrent of water crashing through the narrow gap can be heard a long way off. There are many 'strids' along the rivers of Yorkshire but non so mighty and powerful as the one near Bolton Abbey on the River Wharfe. Its reputation is fearsome with many people being drowned or dragged under by this mighty river when in spate. The temptation to jump across the gap between the rocks across the thundering torrent is for the foolhardy but standing there I have to admit I was tempted to make the death defying leap. I didn't, and am here to tell the tale but there are many who have perished at the mighty Wharfe Strid. Please do not yield even if the river is flowing gently as it is very deep and has lots of undercurrents even when it looks calm and gentle. The Strid has a lot to answer for in these parts as legend says it was the indirect reason why the magnificent Bolton Abbey was built. In the 12th century the Romille family were rich landowners in Yorkshire. Their only surviving son, known as the 'Boy of Egremond', was keen on walking the woods thereabouts with his hound looking for deer. Hundreds of times he had approached the Strid and with a mighty leap would safely land on the rocks at the other side. But one day his hound, its lead attached firmly around the boys hand, decided not to jump. The boy was deposited into the Wharfe and drowned. Legend says that because of this terrible disaster his parents gave land for the building of Bolton Priory in his memory. I believe this is a fine tale but records prove that the transaction was done before the Boy of Egremond was drowned! However, the fact remains that the boy was drowned at the Strid and Bolton Abbey was built.

The Facts
Distance - 3 miles (4.8km)
Time - 1 Hour
Start/Parking - Bolton Abbey GR 071539.
Park along the river side at the Pavilion
Map - OS Outdoor Leisure 10
Refreshments - Café at the Pavilion at the start
Public Toilets - At start and at the Pavilion

Your Route

This is a short walk to be included whilst spending a day by the riverside at Bolton Abbey. It is easy with good paths and very little navigation. If you wish to be adventurous you may continue along the river side path past the Strid and cross the bridge higher up stream to return on the other side of the river.Or simply return the way you came through the woods. From the main road enter the grounds of Bolton Abbey at the Pavilion car park and park along the river bank. Walk towards the Pavilion passing it by to enter the woods through a gate. Continue straight ahead along the good path taking the opportunity to read the information board as you pass. To make your route easier choose the coloured waymarks from the information route guide to visit the Strid. Look out for Heron along the way it is a favourite stretch of river for these wily fishermen. You will hear the roar of the Strid as you approach, please keep well clear of the water and the slippery rocks nearby, view it from a distance. Return the same way you came or take the alternative as mentioned earlier.

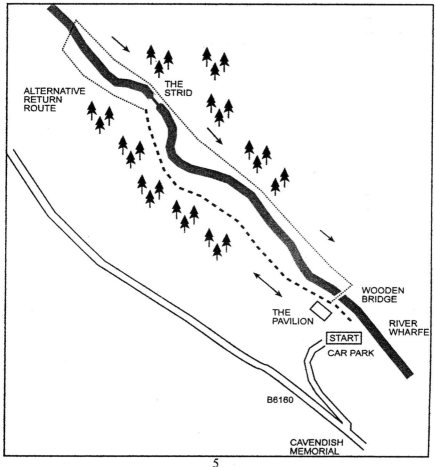

A SHORT WALK TO LINTON FALLS

L inton Falls are magnificent when the River Wharfe is in flood. The water crashes over the wide but low drop of the higher falls then pours noisily over the lower falls before thundering across the rocky exit under the bridge. If they are magnificent when in flood they are almost musical and serene in drier times. An added benefit of this short route is a walk up to Ghastrill's Strid which is a good picnic area. Unfortunately you will have to return from the strid the same way you came as far as the bridge on the Threshfield road. There are many other public footpaths on which you should be able to return to Grassington but I am afraid they are difficult and un-marked. The walk is only short, if you wish to extend the walk the footpath continues past the strid area to eventually meet the road.

The Facts

Distance - 2½ miles (4km) or 4 miles (6.4km)
Time - An hour or two depending if you extend the
walk or not
Start/Parking - Grassington. GR 922876.
Pay & Display car park at entrance to village
on the B6265 from Hebden
Map - OS Outdoor Leisure 10
Refreshments - Cafes, pubs, sandwich shop and a
bakers exist in the village
Public toilets - In the car park

Your Route

L eave the car park at the main entrance then turn right. In a few yards turn right again along a lane at a sign for Linton Falls. Walk along the lane eventually keeping to a narrow enclosed path leading downhill to the falls passing through a couple of gates along the way, you should be able to hear the roar of the falls by now. At the bridge enjoy the view of the falls but do not cross. The path is through a stone stile on the right before the bridge to reach the river bank signed to Grass Wood.

After the second falls bear right across the field on a worn path which leads to the road and bridge. Cross the road and take the wide track opposite leading downhill to a gate into a field signed to Wood Lane to return to the river bank.

Continue along the river bank passing through gates and eventually onto a stony area by the river. Bear right now onto a stony path then through a stone squeeze stile. In a few yards pass through another stone stile into an overgrown area. Pass the strid and enter an open area over a wooden stile. If you wish to go further you may continue along the footpath to the road. If not retrace your steps as far as the road bridge then turn left through a stile before the road at the sign for Wood Lane. Climb uphill now keeping straight ahead through the houses to a crossroad. Turn right here to reach Grassington shopping area. Then follow sign for National Park to return to the car park.

- - - o 0 o - - -

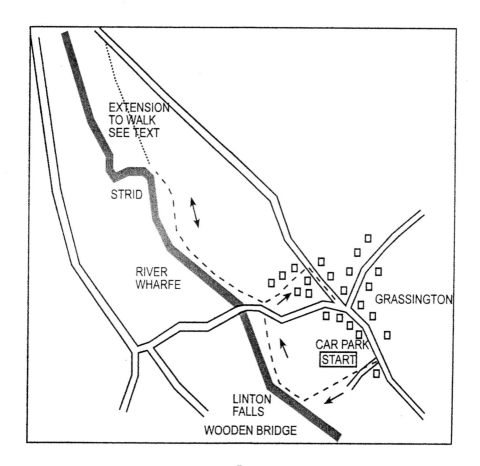

OLD GANG SMELTING MILL

The beauty of the Yorkshire Dales village of Langthwaite in Arkengarthdale in the spring is only exceeded by the impressive rich colours of Autumn. Approaching from Reeth with Fremington Edge on the right and Calver Hill on the left Langthwaite presents itself as a peaceful green oasis in a wild and bleak landscape. Mining was prominent in the surrounding hills and it is on an old mining road that we walk to explore ruins of days gone by. You can feel the atmosphere as you walk along the old tracks with just the ghosts of long gone miners for company. All that remains of the derelict buildings are an unsafe mass of stone and twisted steel. But if you stop for a while and let your imagination drift back in time you might hear the voices of the miners and the thunder of the machinery around the Smelting Mill! After passing the main area of the mill the route leaves the valley to traverse Reeth High Moor where there are more reminders of mining - slag heaps! So many that the path is marked with cairns and posts to guide you through the maze. At all times keep to the bridleway as there are many old mine shafts in the area.

The Facts
Distance - 6 miles (9.6km)
Time - 2½ hours
Start/Parking - Surrender Bridge on the Arkengarthdale to Swaledale road. GR 989999. Waste ground used as parking area alongside the road at Surrender Bridge
Maps - OS Outdoor Leisure 30
Refreshment - The pub at Langthwaite is highly recommended but is some way from the walk

Your Route

If you are approaching from Arkengarthdale Surrender Bridge is two miles along the road at the second double bend/dip in the road. Cross the road from the parking area onto an obvious wide bridleway keeping Old Gang Beck on your left. Eventually the track falls to the ruins of the Old Gang smelting mill alongside the beck. There is much of interest here if you like mining relics, many parts of the machinery were simply left where they stood. Be careful though, it is unsafe to enter the old buildings. Continue along the track past the working area and keep right at the junctions to eventually join a deteriorating, narrower track. Follow this track round to the right across the beck, re-crossing the same beck later to pass through a gate with bridleway waymarks nearby. Uphill now seemingly for ever as the bridleway gently climbs onto the moor. You must follow the cairns and thread your way between the slag heaps. If you enjoyed the shelter of the Old Gang Beck valley you will find it can become a little breezy and cold as you traverse Reeth High Moor. Eventually you reach a large slag heap at the summit of the moor with a cairn on top. Fantastic views from here across to Calver Hill in the east. You must bear right now along a track with another cairn to guide you away from the slag heaps. Keep to the track though as there is a peat bog on your right - look how the water seeps out into the ditch! It's all downhill from here as the wide track winds its way to the road. Turn right at the road and in about half a mile return to Surrender Bridge

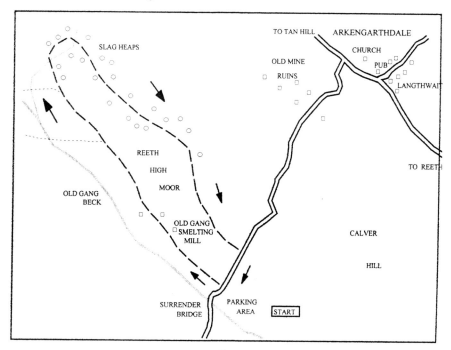

FREMINGTON EDGE

The village of Fremington gets its name from the 'Fremings', an ancient name for foreigners, they lived outside the boundaries of the Angles who had a settlement nearby. Now we are the foreigners as we walk around Fremington and the little town of Reeth. The wide bridleway climbs steeply to the top of Fremington edge along the gullies and slagheaps of the old lead mines. From the summit the savage beauty along Arkengarthdale and the tiny community of Booze adds to the scenic splendour of the walk.

The Facts

Distance - 7.5 miles/12km

Time - 4 hours

Start/Parking -. Start from Reeth Post Office adjacent to the village green. GR 039993. You may park around the green or follow signs to the car park

Map - OS Landranger 98 + 92 or OS Outdoor Leisure 30

Refreshments - There are six cafes, three pubs and a sandwich shop in Reeth

Public toilets - At the top of the village green at Reeth

Your Route

Start from the Post Office and walk towards the Ivy Cottage Tea Rooms. Passing the Arkelside Hotel on your right follow the narrow road which bends to the right downhill. When the road bends to the left keep straight ahead onto the footpath at the sign. The pleasant river side walk exits at the bridge. Pass under the bridge then right and right again to cross the bridge on the road. Turn right once over the bridge, cross the road and enter a field through a squeeze stile. Turn immediately left to a gate with a white arrow then continue along and past the right hand side of a barn towards the two large trees and through the stile. Bear right and over a hillock then right through a stile and immediately left across the field to a gateway with a yellow marker. Continue uphill to a gate. Follow the rough track as it descends towards the river, eventually to a field. Bear slightly right here and exit the field across a broken wall towards the hawthorn bushes. Climb steeply for 30yds then bear right uphill towards the gateposts. Ignore the path going into the wood. Through the gateway then over a wall and left onto an old mining track. Walk through the wood and descend to a signpost. Through the gate walk slightly right up-hill in the direction of the bridleway sign. Pass confirmation waymarks on your way to a gate. Through the gate continue on the obvious path passing the odd farmhouse on the left to a gate with a yellow waymark. The path becomes stony now and climbs to the right through nettles. Then through a gate and descend following the waymarks to pass behind a house and onto the drive. Ignore the signpost and continue straight ahead to a gate. Cross the field to the gateway opposite and soon exit the field to pass behind the farmhouse along a lane. At the next house turn right along a wide track signed 'BP Hurst'. This is the start of the steep climb up to Fremington Edge with fantastic views along Arkengarthdale and to Booze. Keep on the wide track following a sign and lots of waymarks all the   way to the top where you are then guided by cairns to a gate.

Keep straight ahead through the gate close to the wall on your right as the path now falls slightly and after a walk of about a mile and a half you arrive at a fence. Turn right here through the gate onto a stony mining road and descend to the village of Fremington with stimulating views across the dale to Reeth. At the houses the road bends right then left. At the left bend bear right onto a wide track to a squeeze stile and gate. Through the stile bear left away from the farm track keeping close to the wall on the left. Downhill now to pass through three squeeze stiles to follow an obvious path to exit onto the road at Reeth Bridge. Take the same riverside path you came on or the road-side footpath to return to Reeth.

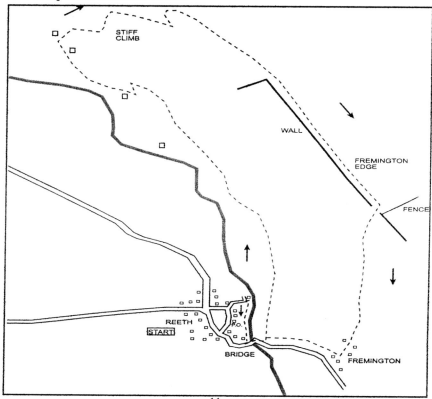

A SHORT WALK TO HIGH FORCE

*H*igh Force is one of the lesser waterfalls in the Yorkshire Dales and is surrounded by trees. Access is limited to peering down on it from the roadside. However, it is a fine sight after heavy rain and the thunderous noise it makes as it tears down the hillside can be heard as you approach from quite a way off. The route is undefined in places and returns along the quiet Blean Lane passing High Blean Farm then Low Blean Farm as the road descends to Semerwater. The views on the return are fantastic across a tranquil Semerwater to Raydale and its surrounding fells. I am afraid there is not a refreshment stop this time but at least you can have a paddle in Semerwater on your return!

The Facts
Distance - 3 miles (4.8km)
Time - A good hour
Start/Parking - Park on the shore of Semerwater, currently a fee of £1.00 per full day, 50p for three hours, is payable at Low Blean Farm 400yds. along the road. Grid. ref. 922876
Map - OS Outdoor Leisure 30
Refreshments - None

Your Route

Start from the car parking area along the shore of Semerwater not forgetting to pay your car park fee at Low Blean Farm if you didn't pay as you passed on the way there. Turn left and head off in the direction of Semerwater Bridge. Cross the stile at the bridge into the field on the right signed to Bainbridge. A pleasant walk along the bank of the River Bain takes you to a stile into another field. At the following stile do not cross but turn right as indicated by the bridleway sign pointing uphill to Blean Lane.

Climb the grassy bank to a gate. Through the gate and sign for Blean Lane keep straight ahead close to the wall on the left to another gate. Pass through the gate now keeping close to the wall on the right to eventually exit the field through a gate (or over if the gate is tied). Bear right now on a stony path climbing across the field. The stony path expires into the grass but keep straight ahead to soon meet up with the farm drive. Go left onto the drive and climb steadily to the road. At the road turn right along Blean Lane still climbing. Fabulous views across Semerwater and along Raydale present themselves in front of you now. As the Lane falls downhill you should be able to hear the

roar of High Force below you in the trees if it is full of water.
As you cross the bridge peer over to take a look at High force then continue
along past a couple of farms. Eventually the road bends to the right, follow it
right round to go steeply downhill back to the car parking area at Semerwater.

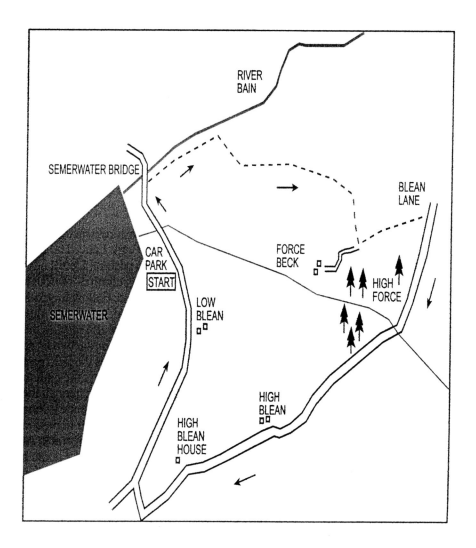

HISTORIC GRASSINGTON

*G*rassington is a superb place to start the walk. It has one of the larger Dales car parks with toilets and a Tourist Information Centre. On return there is a good choice of refreshment with cafes, pubs and a sandwich shop. In its early days Grassington was an important Iron Age settlement but its main growth area was in lead mining which gave it a surge in population. As you climb above Grassington you pass through an ancient field system.

The Facts

Distance - 6.5 miles/10.5km

Time - 3 hours

Start/Parking - Grassington. GR 003639. Pay & Display car park at entrance to village on the B6265 from Hebden

Map - OS Outdoor Leisure 10

Refreshment - Cafes, pubs and a sandwich shop in Grassington

Public Toilets - In the car park

Your Route

Start in the village square and walk uphill past the Devonshire Arms. Shortly turn left into Chapel Street and eventually right up Bank Lane. The lane bends right and in a few yards goes left over a stile into a pasture. Uphill now with confirmation footpath signs along the way. After a long climb exit through a squeeze stile. Straight ahead then slight right to a large stile. Follow footpath signs then over a stone stile and on an obvious path to a ladder stile passing through the ancient field system. Keep on the narrow path uphill ignoring the wide grassy track on the left to a wall with a gate stile. Head for the two large ice age stones at the top of the hill. Over a ladder stile then across the field past an old dry pond on the left and over a difficult stone stile. Follow the path to yet another stile then bear right to shortly join a farm road. Go left here all the way to a derelict stone barn passing the sign for 'Footpath to Conistone' along the way at the gate. At the barn turn right through the gate then left to pass in front of it. Approach the farmhouse then turn right on a wide grassy track. At the farmhouse gate there is a signpost pointing in this direction saying 'Footpath to Conistone'. Downhill now with fantastic views ahead, it is quite steep at times. At the second gate which is identified by two narrow gateposts bear slightly left downhill through a rocky environment. Exit over a ladder stile and soon pass through a small gate. Continue straight ahead on the narrow track. At the wall make an acute left turn signed as 'Footpath to Grassington', do not pass over the stile! Cross open land to a ladder stile then downhill to a well maintained lime kiln, a good place to eat your sandwiches on a rainy day. Keep on downhill with limestone pavement to your right. Pass over a ladder stile then left through a gate. Still downhill to another ladder stile then bear left to a stone squeeze stile, then another. Go left along the line of the wall now to corner and squeeze stile with a sign 'Footpath to Grassington'. Pass through a gate and a footpath sign then into a farm yard. Follow path through the farm yard as directed by signs to the road. Keep straight ahead now to return to Grassington for some refreshment.

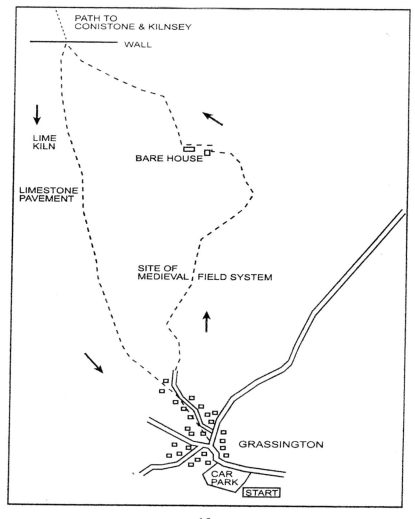

SWALEDALE & CRACKPOT HALL

Crackpot Hall, a farmhouse built on the side of a hill with stunning views of upper swaledale is now a ruin. The walk passes to the rear of the hall across the remains of mining operations and climbs past another old building, a smithy from the mining days, and along to Swinnergill. Apart from mining there were devious religious goings on in these parts many years ago! The return route along the precipitous sides of Swinnergill is exciting and rewarding, good footwear is essential. If heavy rain has swelled the gill it will not be possible to cross, see route description for an alternative.

The Facts
Distance - 7.5 miles/12km
Time - 3½ hours
Start/Parking - Muker. GR910979. Park in village car park adjacent to bridge on road from Gunnerside
Map - OS Outdoor Leisure 30
Refreshment - Café and pub in the village

Your Route

Leave the car park at Muker turning left across the bridge. Soon take the first turning to the right into the village Keep right past the Post Office and go left at Corner Cottage along a lane signed to Gunnerside and Keld. Soon pass through a squeeze stile at the footpath sign. Continue along through several stiles and meadows along a flagged path eventually passing through a gate and down stone steps to the River Swale. Go left here along a rocky path following the sign for footpath. Soon leave the rough path through a stile onto a wide grassy track. Continue straight ahead through several stiles and gates with the river on your right. Eventually the path bears right to the river bank. When it becomes stony bear slightly left away from the river to a squeeze stile in a broken wall. Head for the barns in the distance through more squeeze stiles, some with yellow roundels of paint for waymarks.

Keep straight ahead looking for occasional yellow roundels to guide you eventually climbing up past a couple of barns to a precarious squeeze stile. Some paving now then a stony path up the hill passing another couple of barns with a signpost to Keld hiding behind one of them. Continue climbing and soon take the track between two stone walls. The stony track eventually levels out then descends through a gate into a wood. Soon the path falls to a signpost for the Pennine Way. Keep straight ahead downhill soon passing a sign for Kisdon Force. Continue straight on for a few yards then where the path dips turn right along a steep downhill narrow path. If you reach the gate you have missed the turning! Left at the river then soon right across the footbridge with superb views of the falls. Left over the bridge then immediately right ascending past the falls on your right to a signpost. Turn right here to leave the Pennine Way, cross the stream then right onto an old mine road. Climbing again to a gate then straight ahead with wonderful views of Swaledale. Eventually the path kinks round a barn and shortly after passing the rotting old tractor take the left fork uphill to the ruins of Crackpot Hall. From here must be the best view of Swaledale with Muker in the distance. (*If heavy rain has swelled the rivers you will not be able to cross Swinnergill which lies ahead. Retrace your steps to the previous fork and turn left to rejoin the wide track down into Swaledale.*) Pass behind Crackpot Hall climbing on a wide stoney path and past the old smithy. Exit through a gate then on a tricky path through large rocks. Continue along the descending path. Just before the old mining ruins do a 'U' turn to the right at the signpost for Muker. This is a narrow path with a precipitous drop into Swinnergill, please take care. The narrow path falls to the gill along a precarious rocky descent. Scramble across the large stones to the other side and join another narrow and tricky path climbing up to the right, looking back along Swinnergill the rocky outcrops are dramatic. Eventually the path levels out, becomes wider and descends into Swaledale. At the bottom of the hill bear left along a wide stony track along the river side for about one mile. When the track starts to climb bear right along a narrow path to a footbridge over the River Swale. Cross the river, bear right and in a few yards go left up the stone steps at the signpost to join the flagged paths across the meadows you used at the start to return to Muker.

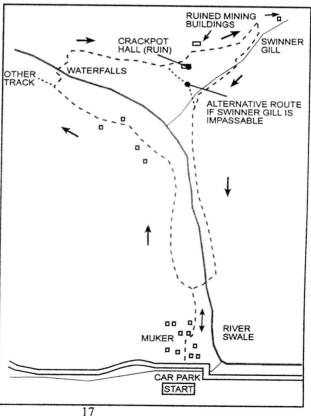

17

BOLTON CASTLE & AYSGARTH FALLS

The grim fortress of Bolton Castle, its walls seven feet thick, was where Mary Queen of Scots spent some of her time imprisoned under the eye of Lord Scrope. However, visitors to the castle are guaranteed a more pleasant reception today and are released after a tour of this impregnable building. After a fine high walk overlooking Wensleydale to the Aysgarth Falls Visitor Centre take time to view these impressive falls. As the River Ure thunders over limestone shelves it flows through remarkable scenery on its way along Wensleydale.

The Facts

Distance - 7.5 miles/12km
Time - 3 hours
Start/Parking - Car park for Bolton Castle in Castle Bolton village. GR 033919
Map - OS Landranger 98 or OS Outdoor Leisure 30
Refreshments - Inside Bolton Castle, The Wheatsheaf pub along the route at Carperby. Visitor centre about half way along the route at Aysgarth Falls
Public Toilets - At the start and at the Aysgarth Falls centre

Your Route

Leave the car park at Castle Bolton not forgetting to drop a coin in the trust the motorist box at the exit. Turn right away from the castle through the gate and head off along a wide track as signed to Askrigg. It is easy to navigate along this track through several gates and the yellow paint waymarks. The track enters open land past the farm buildings as it heads towards Carperby. Soon the track disappears and turns to grass with yellow paint on stones for waymarks. It crosses a small stream which can be difficult if in flood and exits through a gate. Follow the sign for Askrigg and Carperby. At the next gate the track splits. Bear left now signed to Carperby. Soon the path falls steeply all the way to the village with views of the picturesque village of Carperby below you. At the village walk straight ahead to the main road. Turn right and opposite the Wheatsheaf turn left along the public footpath signed to Aysgarth. Soon cross a small stone bridge then after the gate on the right go right through a squeeze stile. Turn immediately left now, cross two fields to exit through a stone stile into a lane. Right at the lane then immediately left across the stile into a field signed to Aysgarth. Straight ahead for 100yds and turn right at the stile. Follow the worn grassy path across several fields and stiles to eventually reach a small gate into a wood. Enter the wood to continue straight on then right and left to go downhill to the road. Left at the road either to the Aysgarth Visitor centre on the right or continue along the road then left at the sign for the falls through a gate into a wood. After visiting Lower Falls continue along to soon leave the wood. Bear left soon at the sign to Castle Bolton on the left and follow the fence to a stile. If you wish to visit the falls do so now then return to this point. Cross the stile and head slightly left to climb up to and exit the field through the gate to Hollins House Farm. Go right past the farmhouse and exit through a gate. In a few yards leave the farm road to turn right onto a wide grassy track at the footpath sign. Continue along past a gate, then a squeeze stile. Follow the worn path across the field into the opposite corner down the hill. Over a stile near a Castle Bolton signpost then a stile and a small gate then keep to the wall on the right as directed by the amusing sign. Eventually enter a leafy lane over a loose stile, take care. After almost 1 mile the grassy lane becomes a tarmac lane at the farm. At the first bend in the lane go left onto the grass verge and over a stone footbridge then left over a stile and a wall into a field. Sharp right now to yet another stile then one more field to cross and exit onto the road over a stile. Cross the road and walk up the road to Castle Bolton and up a steep hill to return to the car park.

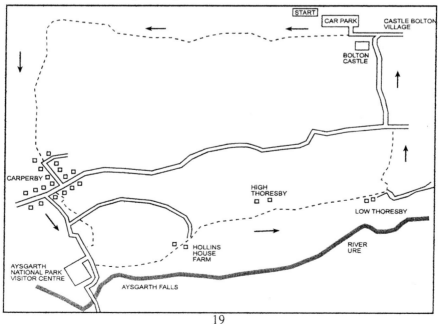

SEMERWATER & BAINBRIDGE

Semerwater nestles amongst the hills which overlook fabulous Wenslydale. The walk takes us along the bank of the River Bain, perhaps the shortest river in England, as it flows out of Semerwater to join the river Ure after a spectacular entrance into Bainbridge - an old fashioned village built around a village green on which stand the village stocks. The Romans had two camps here on the surrounding hills and their road over Wether Fell is still prominent in the west.

The Facts

Distance - 6.5 miles/10.4km

Time - 2.5 hours

Start/Parking - Park on the shore of Semerwater, currently a fee of £1.00 per day, 50p for three hours, is payable at Low Blean Farm 400yds/mtrs. along the road. Grid ref. 922876

Map - OS Outdoor Leisure 30

Refreshments - Rose and Crown at Bainbridge

Public Toilets - In Bainbridge

Your Route

Leave the car park turning left to walk along the road to Semerwater Bridge. Turn right over a gated squeeze stile at the sign for Bainbridge. Follow the river bank, ignoring the bridleway to the right, crossing several stiles and eventually a footbridge. Leave the river bank now as you approach another stile into a field. Cross the middle of the field climbing steadily up Bracken Hill as the River Bain plunges into a narrow valley on the left. Pass through several more squeeze stiles keeping straight ahead still climbing the hill. Crest the hill then bear right to follow the wall down to a squeeze stile. Continue downhill along a wide grassy path passing confirmation signs along the way with good views across to Bainbridge, Wensleydale and Ellerkin Scar in front you. Keep going downhill, ignoring the stile over the wall on the right, until you reach the road.

Bear left now into Bainbridge village. There are a couple of shops in Bainbridge and the Rose & Crown is at the end of the village green just past the toilets which are on the right. The return walk starts at the entrance to the village where you came in along the road signed to Countersett. It is a stiff climb along this quiet road to begin with but it soon eases into a gentle climb. In about 0.6mile the road turns sharp left. Leave the road here to go straight ahead onto the byway which stretches into the distance in front of you and eventually climbs over Wether Fell. It is a long pull across the old Roman Road. In about 2miles the Roman road crosses a modern road. A few hundred yards before this point, just past a large bush look for a gated stile on the left. Pass through the stile and climb diagonally to the left, it is perhaps best to climb fairly steeply as there is no marked path here. (If you missed the stile and arrive at the road go left along the road instead.) When you meet the wall at the top if you cannot see the squeeze stile go left until you do. Exit onto the road then go left for a short way round the bend then enter a field on the left through a gate at the sign for footpath to Countersett. Turn immediately right to walk downhill to the squeeze stile opposite. Continue downhill through a gully then bear left to the wall opposite. Follow the wall downhill until just past the bushes and just before the barn go left through a stone stile. Turn right downhill to exit at the large gate at the bottom of the field adjacent to the barn. Through the gate bear right towards the houses of Countersett passing a footpath sign painted on the fence. Exit onto a farm road a little further along through the gate then turn right at the tarmac road. In a few yards turn left at the crossroads to return to Semerwater.

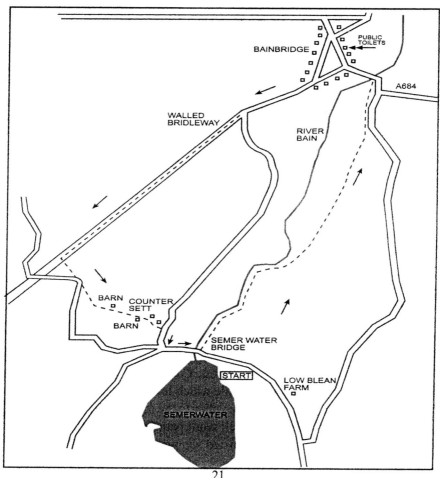

KETTLEWELL AND CAM FELL

Kettlewell, once a market town of some importance famous for its fairs, is now a quiet, sleepy village awakened only by the influx of tourists. The best view of Kettlewell is seen as you ascend the bridleway up to Cam Head. Perhaps the best view of Upper Wharfedale is from the Cam Head track too as it climbs steeply at times to a height of 1725ft. The descent to Starbotton is as severe as the climb, and hard on the knees! The reward is a refreshment stop at the Fox and Hounds Inn before a scenic walk along the bank of the River Wharfe to return to Kettlewell.

The Facts

Distance - 7 miles (11km)

Time - 3½ hours

Start/Parking - Kettlewell, from the dales car park on left or field car park on right entering Kettlewell along the B6160 from Grassington. GR 969723

Map - OS Outdoor Leisure 30

Refreshments - Two pubs and cafes in Kettlewell. The Fox and Hounds at Starbotton about half way along the walk is recommended

Public toilets - In the village at Kettlewell as signed.

Your Route

From the car park walk into the village, cross the bridge at the sign for Buckden then immediately right signed to Coverdale. At the Post Office cross the road to head uphill along the Leyburn road. A very steep climb to a severe left bend then at the sharp right bend leave the road to go straight ahead onto a wide, stony bridleway signed to Starbotton and Coverdale.

The real climb starts now and it is hard going underfoot. The reward is the fine view as you look back across Kettlewell and along Wharfedale to Grassington. As you climb higher you will see in the mid distance the peculiar overhang of Kilnsey Crag come into view. After climbing for some time you reach a gate, stile and a seat to have a welcome rest. Continue along over the stile to eventually reach another gate and stile which leads onto open land, the fine views are now on the right across the valley to the mighty mass of Whernside. Keep straight ahead following a well worn path through a small gate and a short climb on a rocky path to a twisted signpost at Cam Head. Make a 'U' turn left here in the direction of Starbotton and still climbing for a short way as you walk around the end of Cam Head. Pass through a gate as the path starts to fall, soon very steeply and rocky. The fine views ahead are further up Wharfedale towards Buckden and Langstrothdale. Eventually cross a stile then continue down to Starbotton village.

From the track keep straight ahead. At the main road turn right and in a few yards you will find the Fox and Hounds Inn. After refreshment turn back the way you came but this time keep on the main road through the village. At the end of the houses turn right at the sign for Arncliffe, Kettlewell and Buckden along a narrow path leading to a footbridge across the River Wharfe. Cross the bridge and turn left over the stile signed to Kettlewell. Follow signs for Dalesway Footpath crossing stiles as you go. You soon leave the river to cross diagonally right then a short climb through a large gate with a Dalesway arrow. At the next stile bear right towards the stone wall then follow the path straight ahead. Continue along the obvious path and the odd Dalesway sign crossing many stone and ladder stiles. Eventually pass through a small gate on the right to return to the bridge and car park at Kettlewell.

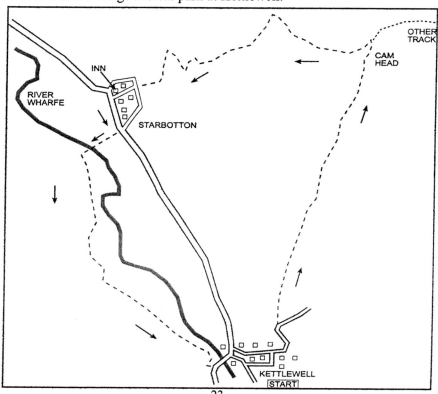

BOLTON ABBEY & BARDEN FELL

Wharfedale is home to Bolton Abbey. Of all the ruins of Abbeys and Priories in the country none are situated amidst such grand scenery as this 12th century Augustinian Priory. The walk climbs up to the summit of Barden Fell with fantastic views along Wharfedale all the way. Returning via Pickles Gill and the tiny hamlet of Storiths. Parking is plentiful and the facilities are good if you pay the fee at Bolton Abbey. However, there is some free parking at Bolton Bridge and you can start the walk from either place.

The Facts

Distance - 6½ miles (10.4km)
Time - 3½ hours
Start/Parking - Bolton Abbey GR 071539 or
Bolton Bridge GR 070531
Map - OS Outdoor Leisure 10
Refreshments - Café in the village and at the Pavillion at the Wooden Bridge. Shop in car park at Bolton Abbey
Public Toilets - At start and at the Pavilion

The Route

Leave the Bolton Abbey car park past the Post Office bearing right into the village and towards the main road. Cross the road in the direction of the priory sign and enter the priory grounds through a gate known as the hole in the wall. Walk through the grounds to the bridge straight ahead and cross the River Wharfe. Look out for the herons, this is a favourite place for them to do a spot of fishing. Take the path uphill away from the river and enjoy the view of Wharfedale and the priory as you climb. Cross a stile and shortly enter into a wood. Exit the wood onto a road, cross the ford then turn immediately left onto a path then right through a stone squeeze stile. The path falls to the river bank now and exits at the bridge over a stile.(The refreshments at the Pavillion are on the left across the bridge.)

Turn right, cross the road and walk along the drive to Bolton Park Farm. This is the start of a long climb. At the farm follow the sign for 'Barden Fell Access Area'. The obvious, wide path winds its way through meadow and several gates as it climbs towards Barden Fell. Finally, pass through a gate with a 'No Dogs Allowed' sign or climb the large stone stile to reach the access area. Take the right fork to the summit of Barden Fell then take the right fork again. It is a pleasant walk across the fell then downhill to Pickles Gill Beck, a good place to eat your sandwiches perhaps. Climb out of the valley and where the path forks go right towards the signposts. Follow signs for Storiths to a stile then stride out over the summit. Keep following signs for Storiths as you walk downhill and enjoy the views along Wharfedale. At the road go right then shortly left along the no through road. Bear right at the sign for 'Bridleway to Bolton Abbey', pass in front of the farmhouse and exit through a small gate onto a narrow path downhill. Soon you overlook the priory. Go right here then left to return to Bolton Abbey and your transport.

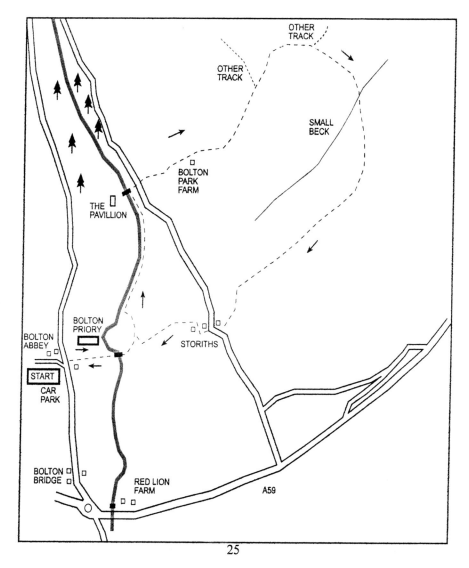

ROUTE 12   WENSLEYDALE
OVER TEN END

Famous for its succlulent Wensleydale cheese the factory at Hawes has an excellent cafe and cheese shop which I recommend you visit on your return. The start of the walk is a stiff climb all the way from Hawes to the summit of Ten End and is best walked on a summers afternoon and evening when you will enjoy the low angle of the sun over the Wensleydale, Sleddale and Widdale landsacape. Wether Fell at 2000ft stands prominent to the east and the even higher Dodd Fell to the west. Perhaps the most dramatic view is past Hawes and along Wensleydale which contrasts with the high fells to the north and the Buttertubs pass.

This route climbs over 'Ten End` which stands at over 1800ft giving superb views all the way. But the return over Cam Road, a rough, rocky descent can be hard on the feet and limbs.

The Facts

Distance - 7 miles (11km)

Time - 3 hours

Start/Parking - Hawes. GR 873898

Map - OS Outdoor Leisure 30 or OS Landranger 98

Refreshments - Cafes, pubs, takeaways in Hawes

Public toilets - In the car park

- - - o O o - - -

Your Route

Leave Hawes on the Sedbergh road and just after the garage turn left along the B6255 signed to Ingleton. Uphill now, then turn left opposite the Honeycott caravan site along a narrow road. In about a quarter of a mile turn right at the second junction on the right signed 'Pennine Way'. The track is wide and stony. At the entrance to Gaudy Farm go slightly left into the field as directed by the 'Pennine Way' sign. Keep close to the wall on the right climbing steeply up the grassy hill. Pass through several gates continuing along the track which becomes quite rough and boggy at times. Continue climbing ever upward towards the summit of 'Ten End' along the obvious track. At the top, pass through another gate keeping to the ridge and to the right of the broken down wall.

Soon you meet a wide, rough track/road, Cam Road. Turn abruptly right onto this and enjoy a downhill walk with superb views past Hawes into the distance. Soon you meet the road, turn right to return down the hill to Hawes.

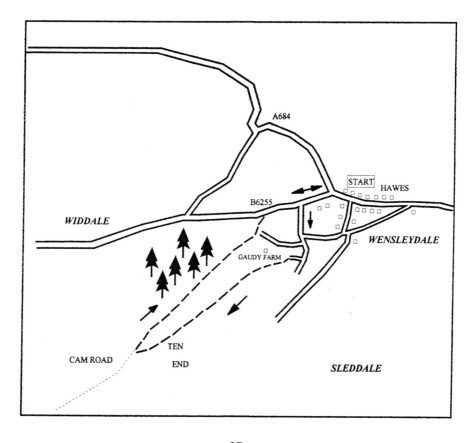

OTHER TRAILBLAZER BOOKS

Mountain Biking around the Yorkshire Dales
Mountain Biking the Easy Way
Mountain Biking around North Yorkshire
Mountain Biking around Ryedale, Wydale & North York Moors
Mountain Biking on the Yorkshire Wolds
Beadle's Bash - 100 mile challenge route for Mountain Bikers
Mountain Biking in the Lake District
Mountain Biking for Pleasure

Twelve Scenic Walks around Ryedale, Pickering & Helmsley
Ten Scenic Walks around Rosedale, Farndale & Hutton le Hole

Walking on the North York Moors
Walking the Ridges & Riggs of the North York Moors
Short Walks around Yorkshire's Coast & Countryside
Walking to Crosses on the North York Moors
Walking to Abbeys, Castles & Churches
Walking on the Yorkshire Coast
Walking around Scarborough, Whitby & Filey

The Crucial Guide to the Yorkshire Coast
The Crucial Guide to Ryedale and the North York Moors
The Crucial Guide to York & District
The Crucial Guide to Crosses & Stones of the North York Moors

Curious Goings on in Yorkshire

Classic Car Log Books